MW01493524

lonely planet

Toilets
of the
World

**100 STRANGE & SPECTACULAR
THRONES, COMMODES, LOOS, & LATRINES**

Introduction

Welcome to a new edition of *Toilets of the World*. I hope you're sitting comfortably. Frankly, the unprecedented popularity of our first book of terrific toilets caught us with our pants down somewhat. It appears that there are more international toilet spotters out there than we had anticipated, and guide number one was enthusiastically received by restroom readers everywhere. So, here we are with a number two.

Given the fact that we all have to use them, it shouldn't be such a shock that a compendium of curious, classy and confounding public conveniences would pique the interest of so many people. Travellers have a particularly enduring fascination with toilets, because we see so many weird and wonderful examples while out and about exploring. The need to answer nature's call is universal, but every country and culture has a slightly different take on how to facilitate that requirement, which can lead to some very interesting – and occasionally alarming – experiences.

So once again, we have scoured the globe in order to compile an atlas of the planet's most extraordinary outhouses, audacious thronerooms, unique urinals, desolate dunnies, cool cubicles, funny thunderboxes, dramatic johns, crazy cans, posh potties, garish garderobes, wonderful water closets, and lavatories that are laudable or laughable for all manner of reasons, ranging from the historic to the hair-raisingly horrific.

GLOSSARY OF TOILET TERMS

Baños SPAIN, SOUTH/CENTRAL AMERICA

Biffy CANADA

Bog BRITAIN

Can NORTH AMERICA

Choo EAST AFRICA (SWAHILI)

Cludgie SCOTLAND

CR (Comfort Room) PHILIPPINES

Dunny (outside toilet) AUSTRALIA/NEW ZEALAND

Gents (men's toilet) WIDESPREAD

Jacks (men's toilet) IRELAND

John USA

Khazi BRITAIN

Ladies (women's toilet) WIDESPREAD

Latrine FRANCE

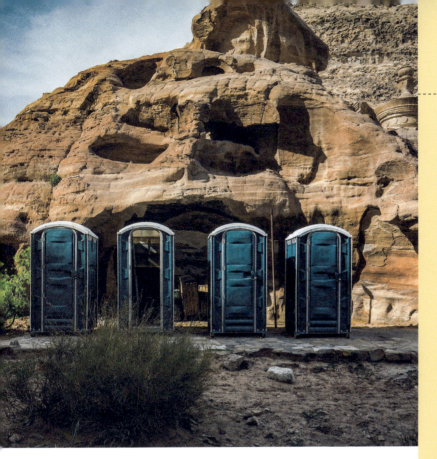

WHERE IS THE TOILET?

ENGLAND
Excuse me, can you direct
me to the toilet please?

AUSTRALIA
G'day mate, where's the dunny?

FRANCE
Excusez-moi, où sont les toilettes?

SPAIN
¿Dónde está el baño?

PORTUGAL / BRAZIL
Onde fica o banheiro?

GERMANY
Wo ist die Toilette?

ITALY
Scusi, dov'è il bagno?

SWEDEN
Var är toaletten?

JAPAN
Toire wa doko desuka?

KOREA
Hwajangsil eodiyeyo?

CHINA (MANDARIN)
Nǎ lǐ Yǒu Cè Suǒ?

EAST AFRICA (SWAHILI)
Choo kiko wapi?

Lavatory BRITAIN

Loo BRITAIN

Outhouse (outside toilet) AUSTRALIA

Pissoir (urinal) FRANCE

Privy BRITAIN

Restroom NORTH AMERICA

Thunderbox (portable toilet) AUSTRALIA

Tŷ bach (small house) WALES

Washroom NORTH AMERICA

WC (Water Closet) ENGLAND

Toilet Timeline

3000 BCE

Toilet trailblazers, Indus Valley, Asia

Houses in ancient cities such as Mohenjo-Daro, Harappa and Lothal in the Indus Valley (modern-day Pakistan and northwestern India) had lavatories connected to sewers and drainage systems in the Bronze Age.

400 BCE

Flushing toilets, Xi'an, China

During a dig in 2023, archaeologists discovered a toilet that they believe was used by an emperor and then flushed manually by servants.

1ST CENTURY CE

Latrines, Ephesus, Turkey

What have the Romans ever done for us? Well, they did design a lot of decent public latrines – including some marble marvels in modern-day Turkey – and then exported the idea all around their empire.

12TH CENTURY

Garderobe, across Europe

French for wardrobe, garderobe also describes the little latrine rooms that poke out of the side of medieval castles, from where waste would fall into a moat, cesspit or upon some unfortunate passerby.

2500 BCE

Take a seat, Eshnunna and Nuzi, Mesopotamia

As far back as 4500 years ago, urbanite Mesopotamians were building brick seats protected by waterproof bitumen over their cesspits.

2000 BCE

Ingenious guttering, Knossos, Crete

The Minoans masterminded sophisticated drains, sewers and systems for separating drinking water (rain) from stinking water (human waste).

1300 BCE

Chamber pots, Egypt

The earliest examples of portable potties for indoor use were unearthed on the banks of the Nile at Tell el-Amarna, the Egyptian capital during the Eighteenth Dynasty.

14TH CENTURY

Wipers, China

The Chinese began mass-manufacturing toilet paper long before the West started wiping – there's even evidence from 1393 showing that perfumed paper sheets were produced for the Hongwu Emperor's imperial family.

1421

Whittington's Longhouse, London

This massive mixed-sex public long-drop toilet with 128 seats opened in central London, from where waste was washed away by the tidal Thames. It was named after Richard Whittington (the real-life Dick Whittington), lord mayor of London, who financed it after discovering the streets were paved with something very different to gold.

1584–91

Ajax, Somerset, England

While in exile from the royal court (for telling rude stories), potty-mouthed poet Sir John Harington invented a flushing toilet and named it 'Ajax'. His godmother, Queen Elizabeth I, was so impressed she forgave him and ordered one for herself.

1857

On a roll, USA

The Western world finally joined the paper chase as Joseph Gayetty of New York began marketing 'Medicated Paper for the Water Closet'. Prior to that, people used old rags, newspapers and magazines.

1848

Loo arm of the law – Westminster, London

A public health act ruled that every new house built in Britain should have a 'WC, privy or ash-pit'.

1880

One good U-turn, Yorkshire, England

Plumber and businessman Thomas Crapper invented the U-bend, stopping gases and bad smells emerging from toilets. Sadly, the connection between his name and the slang word 'crap' is an urban myth.

1775

Out of the closet, London

A flushing-toilet design (very similar to Harington's queen-pleasing Ajax) known as the water closet – leading to the acronym WC – was patented by Alexander Cummings.

1830s

Pissoirs, Paris

Public urinals known as pissoirs first appeared in Paris in the mid-19th century and were subsequently installed in capitals across Europe. Within a century there were more than 1000 pissoirs in the City of Light alone.

1980

The Washlet, Japan

Toto launched a high-tech toilet that not only cleans bottoms with water jets (à la bidets), but also has heated seats that automatically open and close, emits white noise, deodorises the air and features a night light and dryer.

2000

Pop-up potties, the Netherlands

Pioneered in Amsterdam, and now a common feature in modern cities, telescopic toilets hide underground before being elevated to street level during times of high demand (after pubs and clubs shut).

Europe

Loo troll,
Senja, Norway

- - - - - - - - - - - - - - - -

The mountainous isle of Senja in
Troms, northern Norway, home
to Ånderdalen National Park, has
some fantastically futuristic-looking
facilities, but are these toilets
troll proof? (The island echoes
with folkloric tales about these
fantastically frightful creatures.)

Princely privy, Stockholm, Sweden

This impressive *pissoir* (an enclosed urinal in a public space) dates to the late 19th century and still occupies a premium location near the Kungliga Slottet (Royal Palace) in Sweden's capital, Stockholm.

Saltram's throneroom, Plymouth, England

At Saltram House – a Georgian-period mansion full of treasures and antiques in Plymouth, England – even the toilet bowl is made from Royal Doulton china. It's a proper throne (even if the seat is wooden).

Overwater water closet, Thessaly, Greece

Under the boardwalk...is where you do not want to be snorkelling when you're in Thessaly, Greece, at least when this 'bio' bog is in use. Thessaly, called Aeolia in Ancient Greece, features in Homer's *Odyssey* (no mention of the toilet, though).

Taking the piste, Mayrhofen, Austria

When gents take a pee on Mt Penken – a popular destination for adventure-sports enthusiasts above the Alpine village of Mayrhofen in the Austrian Tyrol – they also score a stunning view along the killer Zillertal (Ziller Valley).

Watering the flowers,
Preston, England

Created by San Francisco–based artist Clark Sorensen, this brilliant bunch of flower-inspired urinals at the Barton Grange Garden Centre near Preston, northwest England, are possibly the planet's prettiest porcelain privies.

Parking for beach bums, Costa del Sol, Spain

Resembling beach huts, but with a higher calling, these tidy timber toilet-houses, decked in blue and white, stand tall on a Costa del Sol beach near Marbella in southern Spain.

Teutonic toilet with terrific views, Feldberg, Germany

If your heart has been captured by the Black Forest landscape of Feldberg in southern Germany, don't worry: you don't have to tear your eyes away from it, even when answering the call of nature – at least not in this outhouse.

Wooden water closet, Liverpool, England

The restored Tudor-era interior of Speke Hall, a 500-year-old manor house near Liverpool in England, includes everything from priest-hiding holes to this classic commode, housed within a wonderful wood-panelled room.

Fjordside facilities, Bergen, Norway

Originally built to provide shelter for fisherfolk, many of Norway's traditional *rorbuer* cabins – like this one, by a fjord on the Nordkinn Peninsula in Bergen – are now available as holiday accommodation. Who needs an ensuite bathroom when you have a loo with a view like this?

Designer dunny,
Ureddplassen, Norway

Looking across Norway's mountain-framed
Fugloyfjorden towards the Lofoten Islands, the
Ureddplassen rest-stop bogs along Nordland's
Helgelandskysten scenic road are built to work with
the view and provide a harmonious horizon.

Hadrian's stool,
Northumberland, England

Housesteads Fort in Northumberland was the grandest of all the stations positioned along Hadrian's Wall, which ran right across northern England, but the Roman infantrymen and legionaries who lived there in the 2nd century CE still had to share communal latrines.

Bute's bucket-list bathroom, Scotland

A tiny town on the Scottish Isle of Bute, Rothesay's Victorian-era harbourside toilet block – its century-old urinals resplendent with marble, brass and ceramic features – has become a tourist attraction. King Charles was once the Duke of Rothesay, and a urinal he used bears his coat of arms.

Ultra-cool conveniences,
Dyrhólaey, Iceland

Designed by Reykjavík-based outfit Gláma Kím, these contemporary public loos come with open oceanfront views from the cliffside at Dyrhólaey near Vík, Iceland's most southerly village.

Rainbow restroom, Lisbon, Portugal

Roll with it and pick your toilet paper of choice in these cool and kaleidoscopically colourful Lisbon loos, dubbed the 'Sexiest WC on Earth'. They're located on Terreiro do Paço, one of Portugal's most emblematic and impressive public squares.

A loo to look out for,
Bauska, Latvia

Built in the 15th century above the confluence of the
Mūša and Mēmele Rivers, and used by an order of
Teutonic knights, Latvia's Bauska Castle features a
latrine that protrudes from the wall – certainly one
way to deter would-be attackers.

Deep seat, Gosport, England

If you've ever wondered how to answer the call of nature while underwater, you can find out at the Royal Navy Submarine Museum in Gosport, England, where exhibits include a toilet taken from a real submarine.

Ubercool poo pods, London, England

Fashionably tucked between Soho and Mayfair, Sketch is a tearoom in an 18th-century townhouse by day, and transforms into a cocktail lounge after dark. Its giant egg-like WC spacepods are located under colourful lights in what's possibly London's coolest toilet.

Jazzy gents, Ticehurst, England

The urinals in the gents' loos at the Bell pub in Ticehurst, East Sussex, are not your typical pub bogs – the owners of the English country inn have repurposed a trio of tubas so punters can hit the right note when they start streaming.

Go with the flow, Brittany, France

This historic stone outhouse overhanging the Aven River in the picturesque commune of Pont-Aven in Brittany, France — below a retro advertisement for traditional Traou Mad Breton biscuits — is a much-photographed sight by visitors.

Futuristic Dutch dunnies, IJmuiden

- - - - - - - - - - - - - - -

These toilets look like they've been made to operate on Mars, but they're actually located in the Netherlands province of Noord-Holland – right on the beach at IJmuiden, a port city that straddles the North Sea Canal leading to Amsterdam.

Alpine outhouse, Hohe Tauern, Austria

- - - - - - - - - - - - - - - -

This mountain hut, perched at altitude in the Hohe Tauern Alps, houses a wilderness water closet with a wonderful vista across Carinthia and the sparsely populated wonderland of southern Austria.

Czech...mate,
Prague, Czechia

This judgmental urinal at the Palladium mall in Prague,
the spectacular capital of the Czech Republic, is
definitely not a place for shy guys to hang out.

Old sea bog,
Lelystad, Netherlands

- - - - - - - - - - - - - - -

Sh*t ahoy! Landlubbers can now drop by the
rear toilets on board the *Batavia* – a replica of a
17th-century galleon once commanded by the Dutch
East India Company – by visiting the vessel in the
Netherlands city of Lelystad.

Hide-outhouse,
Matsalu Bay, Estonia

With a roof made from reeds, this natural-looking triangular toilet stands discreetly in Matsalu National Park, Estonia, next to Matsalu Bay, one of Europe's most important wetland areas for birds.

New-look Loos

In Britain, old public restrooms don't really die, they're brought out of retirement and reimagined as bars, theatres and clubs. The following are five of our favourite examples.

Temple of convenience

In the heart of Manchester, England, a disused underground toilet has been redesigned as a subterranean bar (The Temple) with a killer jukebox and a clientele that includes some of the city's most beloved musicians, including Guy Garvey from Elbow, who wrote about this magnetic 'hole in my neighbourhood' in the song 'Grounds for Divorce'.

A wonderful wee theatre

In Newport, South Wales, local woman Janet Martin transformed a derelict gentlemen's conveniences (housed in an Edwardian Grade-II listed building), into a community theatre – the Phyllis Maud Performance Space – where comedians, singers, bands and poets now entertain small audiences.

Caffeine in your cistern

In Fitzrovia, London, artisan coffee shop Attendant occupies a former public toilets that dates to the 1890s. The owners spent two years restoring the restrooms, which still feature original floor and wall tiles along with Doulton & Co porcelain urinals, against which punters now sip their soy lattes below a cistern.

Cocktails and cock tales...

In Kentish Town, north London, another disused toilet is enjoying a new life as an underground cocktail bar called Ladies and Gentlemen, where a mixologist makes magic potions and a jazz pianist can often be found playing the upright in the corner.

Basement jacks

In Shoreditch, London, a former Victorian-era public toilet has been repurposed as an 80-capacity nightclub. The original club – Public Life – lost its licence in 2012 after rowdiness, but the venue reopened in 2022 as The Warmer Room.

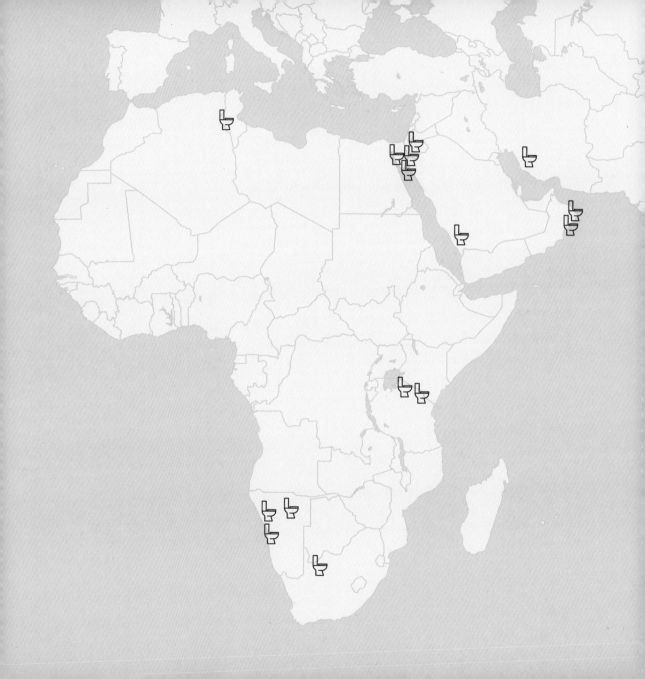

Africa & the Middle East

Outdoor outhouse,
Namibia

Namibia, in southern Africa, is a country full of colour
and contrasts, from arid deserts and vast saltpans
to lush mountain landscapes. This roofless restroom
deep in a verdant part of the Namibian bush is more
comfortable during the dry season.

Going overboard, Oman

Protruding from the side of a traditional Arabian dhow (sailing ship) from Oman, this painted wooden poop deck enables the vessel's sailors to take a long drop right into the ocean.

Luxury loos, Sharqiya Sands, Oman

- - - - - - - - - - - - - - -

The Bedouin have travelled the sandscapes of Oman's Sharqiya Sands, south of Muscat, for centuries – but as tourism makes inroads here, traditional nomadic lifestyles are being altered by modern conveniences like these deluxe facilities.

Can in the sands, Sossusvlei, Namibia

- - - - - - - - - - - - - - -

Namibia is home to Earth's most ancient desert, the Namib, reckoned to be between 55 and 80 million years old and sprinkled by less than 10mm (0.3in) of rain each year. Sensational sand mountains interrupt the horizon around this dunescape dunny.

Khazi in the Kalahari, South Africa

At this loo with a five-star view at South Africa's luxury Tswalu lodge, within a secluded valley in the Kalahari Desert, guests have no nosy (human) neighbours to worry about as they sit and contemplate the savannah grasslands, red dunes and ancient mountains.

Conveniences in the caves, Petra, Jordan

One of the New Seven Wonders of the World, the Rose City rock-houses of Petra, Jordan, housed 20,000 people two millennia ago. Today the site attracts thousands of travellers, for whom modern toilets have been tapered into the rock face.

Desert-view defecation, Damaraland, Namibia

You won't want to stop staring at the fabulous rock formations, desert mountains, petrified forest, exotic wildlife and prehistoric art of Damaraland in Namibia – even when you're on the throne. Luckily, at the Huab Lodge, that's not a problem.

Tanzania's top toilet, Mt Kilimanjaro

- - - - - - - - - - - - - - - -

Towering 5895m (19,340ft) above the East African plains, Mt Kilimanjaro has three volcanic cones. Kibo, the tallest, is dormant but could erupt at any time – something to ponder when you're staring up at it from the toilet in Karanga Camp, 1855m (6086ft) below.

Lofty Egyptian outhouse, Mt Sinai

'Thou shalt not leave the seat up' – the all-important extra rule in this toilet on the flank of Mt Sinai, the mountain on which Moses received the Ten Commandments (according to the Torah, Bible and Quran).

Go alfresco, Wadi Rum, Jordan

Definitely not a throne for agoraphobes (or shy people), this Wadi Rum WC in Jordan doesn't have any water (or even a closet facade), but the views certainly rock.

Divers experience the U-bends, Egypt

Scuba divers exploring the wreck of the *Yolanda* – a cargo ship that came to grief on a reef in 1980 off Ras Mohammed National Park on Egypt's Sinai Peninsula – encounter an incongruous shoal of toilet bowls.

Safari khazi,
Serengeti, Tanzania

- - - - - - - - - - - - - -

From this Tanzanian toilet you can see the Serengeti
from the best seat in the (out) house. Make sure you
flip the sign to 'occupied' so any passing wildebeest
will know they need to queue.

Bog in a box, Serengeti, Tanzania

This may look like a toilet in a tent, but a bog in a box with a flushing cistern constitutes a pretty posh privy when you're on safari in the Serengeti in Tanzania, East Africa.

Mountain-road restroom, Asir, Saudi Arabia

Rising between the Red Sea and a rust-coloured rocky escarpment, Saudi Arabia's Asir region has the country's highest peaks – including Jabal Soudah, which soars to over 3000m (9800ft) – as well as some of the kingdom's most scenically situated toilets.

Wonder closet,
Shiraz, Iran

Featuring a changing room, an octagonal plunge pool
and a garmkhane (hot tub), the hammam (bathhouse)
at the Arg of Karim Khan in Shiraz, Iran, is an ancient
wonder dating to the 1760s – but for toilet breaks,
people visiting the historic citadel-turned-museum
must use these more modern facilities.

Toilet humour,
Chott el Jerid, Tunisia

- - - - - - - - - - - - - - -

If you need the can while visiting the epic Chott el
Jerid salt pans of Southern Tunisia, fear not: the rest
area's deluxe dunnies are surely the most comfortable
seats in the Sahara – it says so right there. (If they
don't live up to expectations, you could always look
around the vast salt lake for an alternative.)

Asia

Toilets by design, Shibuya, Tokyo

- - - - - - - - - - - - - - - - -

Named Nishisando, this Sou Fujimoto–designed convenience just off a major junction in Shibuya is part of the Tokyo Toilet project, which resulted in 16 acclaimed architects and designers transforming 17 public restrooms into inviting, high-tech facilities.

Urinals in the sky,
Osaka, Japan

- - - - - - - - - - - - - - -

It's hard to turn your back on the
stunning view from the upper
floors of Abeno Harukas in Osaka,
until 2023 the tallest building in
Japan, but when needs must...

Snow-proof privy in the peaks, Kyrgyzstan

Fed by a sparkling crown of ice-capped peaks, the Ala-Archa River in Kyrgyzstan flows through a gorge in its namesake national park, where the restrooms are almost as impressive as the incredible alpine views.

Ultra-chic or the stuff of nightmares: Tokyo's trendiest (and most terrifying) toilets

----

Stylish Shibuya in Tokyo, Japan, hosts all 17 of the architect-designed public conveniences featured in Wim Wenders' toilet-themed film *Perfect Days*. Designed by Shigeru Ban, the clever cubicles at this Yoyogi Fukamachi Mini Park loo have walls that transform from transparent to opaque when in use... but do you trust the tech?

Trailside toilet,
Pheriche, Nepal

Poised at 4371m (14,340ft), high above the Tsola River in Nepal's Khumba Valley, this peak-flanked loo in the village of Pheriche, within Sagarmatha National Park, has provided relief for many a trekker caught short on the trails.

Top squat spot, Beijing, China

- - - - - - - - - - - - - -

One's enough at this all-gender toilet in a café on Gulou Dongdajie, a busy part of Beijing with a famous drum tower.

Tubular loos, Byeonsanbando, South Korea

The ultimate toilet rolls – these cabins of convenience
are located in Byeonsanbando National Park, South
Korea, where the mountains meet the water on a
picturesque peninsula poking into the Yellow Sea.

Resplendent restrooms, Nanjing, China

When you need a break from relentless retail therapy while shopping at Nanjing City's Deji Plaza, in east China's Jiangsu Province, the shopping centre's sumptuously decorated facilities provide both refuge and restroom.

Restroom on the rim, Mt Papandayan, Indonesia

- - - - - - - - - - - - - - - -

Visitors to this toilet on a rocky track leading up Mt Papandayan – an active volcano near the city of Bandung in West Java, Indonesia – can blame the eggy aroma on sulphuric gases coming out of the ground, rather than any restroom eruptions.

Potty from the past, Kitakyushu, Japan

A retro privy is one of the exhibits at Japan's toilet-themed Toto Museum in Kitakyushu, where old meets alarmingly new, and items on show include Neo, a motorbike that's fuelled by poo.

Palatial privy, Chiang Rai, Thailand

The spectacular golden toilet at the Wat Rong Khun – a striking modern Buddhist temple in Chiang Rai, Thailand – puts an ornate spin on the idea of going to the throne room.

Restrooms on the roof of the world, Thame, Nepal

The mighty Himalayan peaks of Kangtega and Thamserku overlook these long-drop Zen dens, sitting at roughly 4000m (13,000ft) at the Thame Buddhist monastery, within UNESCO-listed Sagarmatha National Park in Khumbu, Nepal.

When you've got to Goa, India

Blue sky and swaying palm fronds form the ceiling of this open-air washroom in Goa, an idyllic location spectacularly situated on the coast of the Arabian Sea in southwest India. Just watch out for falling coconuts.

Gobi Desert garderobe, Mongolia

No, this is not a mirage; there really are toilets for nomadic travellers needing to take a leak while crossing the barren expanse of the Gobi Desert in Mongolia, which covers an area of around 1.3 million sq km (500,000 sq miles).

Flowery facilities,
Changwon, South Korea

- - - - - - - - - - - - - - -

Even the restrooms are on-theme during the Jinhae
cherry-blossom festival – one of South Korea's most
spectacular spring events – in the southern port city
of Changwon.

In the pipeline, Beijing, China

The public toilets contribute to the distinctive architecture of Beijing's 798 Art District, a former industrial zone turned thriving creative enclave in the capital of China.

Tank top,
Samui Airport, Thailand

At Samui Airport in Thailand, men using the urinal
face a colourful aquarium – which is fine for them,
but the poor fish have a much less enviable view
(thankfully their memories are famously short).

Potty under the palms, Sri Lanka

This spacious, palm-thatched, bright-and-breezy designer bathroom in Sri Lanka really puts the room into restroom.

Considerate conveniences, Ragunan, Indonesia

Boxing clever: a colourful and accessible public toilet for people with disabilities stands next to a similarly striking mobile lactation room for nursing mothers in Ragunan, on the outskirts of Indonesian capital Jakarta.

Bog at the Base Camp, Everest, Nepal

Last pit stop before you reach the roof of the world: this tethered toilet tent is an essential service at Everest Base Camp in Sagarmatha National Park, Nepal.

Outhouses with altitude, Laya, Bhutan

The air is thin at these high-altitude school toilets in the village of Laya, Bhutan, the country's uppermost settlement, sitting at almost 4000m (13,000ft) above sea level.

Leh lavatories,
Ladakh, India

Tourists are attracted to Magnetic Hill, outside Leh in the Indian Himalaya, by a famous optical anomaly that fools bewildered brains into thinking cars are rolling uphill. But the incongruous presence of men's and women's toilets here is certainly no illusion.

Long drop, Ergaki, Siberia

- - - - - - - - - - - - - - - -

When you build an outhouse in Siberia, it needs to be tough enough to handle heavy snowfall. This forest thunderbox in the dump zone beneath the mountains in Ergaki Nature Park – a place known as the 'Russian Yosemite' – is feeling the strain.

Cool Caucasus conveniences, Georgia

These portable potties at Georgia's Gudauri winter resort, perched at almost 2200m (7200ft) on the frozen flanks of the Greater Caucasus mountain range, come to the aid of skiers who need a pee when on the piste.

Famous (and infamous) Toilets

Bates Hotel bathroom

Alfred Hitchcock's groundbreaking 1960 movie Psycho was the first film to ever feature a flushing toilet.

Chamber poser

In 18th-century China, a wealthy salt merchant in Yangzhou became the symbol of decadence after commissioning a golden chamber pot so big he had to climb a ladder to use it.

Turd Reich

Pop to the toilet at Greg's Automotive Repair in Florence, New Jersey, and you could be using a facility once owned by der Führer. Apparently taken from Hitler's private yacht, it ended up in a New Jersey junkyard, where Greg Kohfeldt picked it up.

Ladies don't prefer blondes

The Knickerbocker Hotel in Los Angeles was once a famous haunt for Hollywood stars, but according to some stories, in true Hotel California style, some could never leave. Allegedly, the ghost of Marilyn Monroe hangs out in the main floor ladies.

Regal restroom

While Henry VIII had his own toilet (and a wiper, 'the groom of the stool'), the king had a communal toilet constructed for his couriers at Hampton Court in London. Called the Great House of Easement, it was located by the river and could accommodate 14 people in one sitting.

Pain in the butt

According to the 12th-century English historian Henry of Huntingdon, Edmund II, king of England, was sitting on the toilet when he was killed in 1016 by an assassin who had hidden beneath the latrine with a spear.

Taking the pissoir

In 1917, French artist Marcel Duchamp scribbled 'R Mutt' on a porcelain urinal, called the piece Fountain and attempted to exhibit it at the Grand Central Palace in New York.

In space, no one can hear you poo

The Russian-designed toilet onboard the International Space Station cost a cool $19m. Besides combating zero gravity, its fancy functions include the ability to separate solids from urine and turn the latter into filtered drinking water.

Death on the throne

Elvis Presley, popularly known as The King, suffered a cardiac arrest and died on the toilet of Graceland, his Memphis home, on 16 August 1977, aged 42.

Going for gold

Inspired (ironically) by Lenin, who said the best use for gold was building public toilets, the entire bathroom at the Hang Fung Gold Technology showroom in Hong Kong was constructed with solid 24-carat gold – including a flushing toilet – worth a whopping $29m.

Oceania

Jungle john, Kiriwina, Papua New Guinea

When nature calls on Kiriwina, one of the Trobriand Islands – an archipelago of coral atolls that splay in a 450-sq-km (174-sq-mile) arc off the east coast of Papua New Guinea – this discreet leafy lavatory has you covered.

Royal flush, McLaren Vale, South Australia

At d'Arenberg vineyards in the McLaren Vale region of South Australia, the surrealist d'Arenberg Cube is a five-storey multi-function building that seems to float above the Mourvèdre vines – and its urinals are jaw dropping.

Palmerston North's Art Deco dunnies, New Zealand/Aotearoa

Nearby Napier is known as the 'Art Deco Capital of the World', but these public conveniences on the main square in lesser-known Palmerston North, New Zealand, are a classic of example of the architectural style popular in 1930s, when several North Island cities were rebuilt after a massive earthquake.

Outback (tin) can, Western Australia

No need to queue at these tin toilets standing in the red dust of Western Australia, a state about the same size as Western Europe, but home to fewer than three million people, of whom 2.8 million live in the capital, Perth.

Classy Kiwi conveniences, Auckland, New Zealand/ Aotearoa

Located by Auckland's iconic Grafton Gully–spanning Grafton Bridge, and beautifully designed as a single-storey Edwardian baroque building by Walter Ernest Bush (the architect responsible for the bridge), the public loos and former tram shelter on Symonds Rd were the city's first public toilets with facilities for women when they opened in 1910.

Tongariro lunarscape lav, New Zealand/Aotearoa

This camouflaged cubicle of convenience on the route of the terrific Tongariro Alpine Crossing is designed to blend right in to the otherworldly volcanic landscape of Tongariro National Park on New Zealand's North Island.

Wild Otago water closet, New Zealand/Aotearoa

Even the dunnies are delightful on the Catlins River Track, a pleasant 12km (7.5-mile) trail in the Otago region of New Zealand's South Island.

Backwoods thunderbox, Mungo National Park, Australia

Before taking a pew, it's wise to check for spiders under the seat at this wilderness WC in UNESCO World Heritage–listed Mungo National Park, near Balranald in New South Wales, Australia.

Gilded garderobe, Maryborough, Australia

It may not have been graffitied by Michelangelo or exert quite the pulling power of the Vatican, but the 'Cistern Chapel' by Hungarian artist Akos Juhasz in a public toilet block next to Maryborough City Hall in Queensland, Australia, is a spiritual experience.

Sitting pretty, Mt Aspiring, New Zealand/Aotearoa

- - - - - - - - - - - - - - - - -

The tramp to Liverpool Hut in New Zealand's Mt Aspiring National Park is notoriously gnarly, with some seriously precipitous sections, but it's worth it for the view from the loo alone.

The Americas

Toilet tags, Brooklyn, USA

Less stink, more ink: this richly graffitied washroom resides at LowBrow Artique, a gallery and art-supply shop in the ubercool area of Bushwick in Brooklyn, New York.

Pastel pit stop,
Newfoundland, Canada

These colourful public conveniences are in Cow Head on the island of Newfoundland, Canada. The town, with a population of just under 400 people, is blessed with an immense beach looking out over the Gulf of St Lawrence.

Presidential poo pew,
Springfield, USA

- - - - - - - - - - - - - - - -

At the Lincoln Home National Historic Site in
Springfield, Illinois, where Abraham Lincoln lived
before becoming US president, you can visit Abe's
actual outhouse. But which of the potties did he
prefer, and why have three in the first place?

BC's Bugaboo bog, Canada

If you don't mind feeling more than a little exposed, this long-drop loo with a view offers a stunning perspective of the Bugaboo mountain range in eastern British Columbia, Canada.

Colombian conveniences, Quindío

Considering the diuretic and laxative effects that caffeine can have, it's a good job these colourful water closets at the Recuca Recorrido de la Cultura Cafetera, deep in Colombia's UNESCO-listed Coffee Cultural Landscape, are in such fine condition.

Rocket can, Huntsville, USA

- - - - - - - - - - - - -

Doing your business in zero gravity sucks – just ask an astronaut. At the US Space & Rocket Center in Huntsville, Alabama, you can see this space toilet, learn how the vacuum-cleaner-like machine works – and discover what happens to the waste afterwards.

Tropical toilet vibes, San Agustín Lanquín, Guatemala

For guests at this Guatemalan hostel at San Agustín Lanquín, in the central Alta Verapaz department, climbing the steps up to the colourful water closet must feel like taking to the stage.

Blessed relief at temporary toilets, Brooklyn, USA

For runners taking on the challenge of the New York City Marathon, these strategically placed cubicles in Brooklyn offer an opportunity for some restroom redemption.

Ladies & gentoos, D'Hainaut, Antarctica

Tuxedo-attired members of the gentoo penguin population of Antarctica's D'Hainaut Island, on the Palmer Archipelago, can (and do) poo wherever they please, but human visitors are expected to use the extremely cool refuge outhouse.

Pew with a view, Mt Whitney, USA

A potty on the peak of California's Mt Whitney – the mightiest mountain in the contiguous US, at 4421m (14,505ft) – provides a seat in the clouds from where to contemplate the majesty of the Eastern Sierra range.

Pacific Crest Trail pit stop, Donomore Cabin, USA

An emphatic 'engaged' sign hangs on the toilet hut at the historic Donomore Cabin at Klamath River, California, along the epic Pacific Crest Trail, which runs for 4265km (2650 miles) through the Cascade and Sierra Nevada Mountains.

Rockstar toilets, Death Valley, USA

A pair of alfresco outhouse cans lie behind a boulder in Butte Valley, within California's Death Valley – the lowest, hottest and driest national park in the USA, famous for its wildflowers, ghost towns and historic gold and silver mines.

Grand can,
Colorado, USA

On a secret beach at a curve of
the Colorado River, deep within
Grand Canyon National Park,
explorers can take a pew on a
cool commode and watch one of
the world's best-known waterways
flowing past.

Perilous privy,
San Blas Islands, Panama

There are strong pirate vibes to this toilet, located in
the remote San Blas Islands off the Caribbean coast
of Panama, where you have to walk the plank to
reach a precariously positioned potty.

Going green, San Miguel Dueñas, Guatemala

Want a sweet-smelling bathroom? Take a leaf from this plant-filled public toilet within the verdant surrounds of the eco-focused Valhalla Macadamia Farm in San Miguel Dueñas, Guatemala.

Patagonian potty, Torres del Paine, Chile

Even the toilets in Torres del Paine National Park, Chilean Patagonia, are picturesque, but if too many trekkers frequent this wobbly WC, balanced on a wooden jetty over Laguna Azul, the lake risks turning another colour altogether.

Salt lake sitty, Coqueza, Bolivia

This brilliant *baño* in the Bolivian village of Coqueza overlooks the sensational Salar de Uyuni, the biggest salt playa on the planet, covering an incredible 10,582 sq km (4086 sq miles).

Restroom at the end of the universe, Big Bend, Texas

A panoply of planets and stars hangs in the heavens above this lonely outhouse in Big Bend National Park, Texas, where adventure-seekers flock to find fossils and explore endless desert and mountain trails.

Log bogs,
Banff, Canada

In Canada's Banff National Park,
you can explore over 1600km
(1000 miles) of hiking trails, and
choose from 2468 pitches across
13 campsites. And with log-cabin
lavatories like these, below a peak
in the Canadian Rockies, there's
no need to make like a bear.

White Sands water closets, New Mexico

A tidy toilet stands stark against the dazzling dunes and bizarre backdrop of White Sands National Park, where the lunar-like landscape is formed by gazillions of gypsum deposits spread across 710 sq km (275 sq miles) of New Mexico.

Frozen outhouse, Crater Lake, Oregon

When visiting the facilities at the lodge in Oregon's
Crater Lake National Park in winter, take a shovel.
The park is home to the deepest lake in the US,
an immense puddle in the collapsed caldera of
Mt Mazama, an extinct volcano.

Potties in the peaks,
Peruvian Andes

- - - - - - - - - - - - - - - -

For tired trekkers tackling the spectacular but
strenuous 10 to 12-day Cordillera Huayhuash circuit
in the Peruvian Andes, these toilet huts high in the
range are restrooms in every sense of the word.

The bear necessities,
Pictured Rocks, USA

A backwoods bathroom (minus the bath...and the room) in a campground within Pictured Rocks National Lakeshore, where Lake Superior laps at sandstone cliffs, caves and beaches along Michigan's beautiful, forest-fringed (and black-bear-stalked) Upper Peninsula.

Acadian ablutions, New Brunswick, Canada

- - - - - - - - - - - - - - - -

For a window into Acadian culture, stay at Hôtel Château Albert on the Acadian Peninsula in New Brunswick, Canada. Designed by architect Nazaire Dugas in 1907, the original burned down in 1955 but has been painstakingly restored, right down to the toilets.

Altiplano amenities, Siloli Desert, Bolivia

An enormous South American tableland, the Altiplano is an arid, high-altitude expanse, mostly within Bolivia. The Lago Poopó here may have permanently dried up in 2015, largely thanks to climate change, but pooping remains a possibility at these Bolivian bathrooms in the plateau's Siloli high desert.

Going to extremes

Most extreme

The title of the world's most extreme toilet has been awarded to an adrenaline-inducing long-drop in a freezing-cold weather station called Kara-Tyurek in the Altai Mountains of Siberian Russia. The outhouse hangs precariously over a cliff at 2600m (8500ft) above sea level.

Biggest bowl

In Kidscommons, a children's museum in Columbus, Indiana, USA, the World's Largest Toilet (part of the ExploraHouse exhibit) can fit several small people within its behemoth bowl. When the flush is operated it works as a water slide, so you can quite literally drop the kids off at the pool...

Most massive footprint

At the Foreigners' Street amusement park in Chongqing, China, the Porcelain Palace is a massive complex with more than 1000 toilets and urinals sprawling across 3000 sq m (32,000 sq ft). The façade has an ancient Egyptian theme, while another toilet complex to the south invokes the style of Catalan architect Antoni Gaudí, because, well... why not?
➜

Highest

Poo is a problem around Camp Four on Everest's South Col (7906m/25,938ft above sea level), where there are no toilets and climbers just go in the snow. Further down, at Base Camp (5364m/17,598ft), there are proper potties.

Tallest

Stabbing 829.8m (2722ft) into the Dubai sky, the Burj Khalifa is the planet's tallest building, and it boasts the world's highest restrooms in a human-made structure. The crapper in the clouds on the 154th floor (585m/1919ft) is surrounded by windows.

Most remote

In orbit an average of 400km (248 miles) above our heads, the International Space Station (ISS) has space loos in its Zvezda, Nauka and Tranquility units, including a titanium toilet that cost $23m to develop.

Deepest

Well over 2000m (6500ft) below the surface of the planet, at SNOLAB – an underground research laboratory in Greater Sudbury, Ontario, Canada – are four flush toilets, the deepest dunnies on (in) Earth.

Lowest

The Dead Sea is the lowest place on the planet, and if visiting the lowest latrine in the world is on your bucket-list, then you can queue for the loo at Amman Beach on the Jordanian side of the super salty sea, or Ein Bokek Beach on the Israeli shore.

Oldest

Discovered by archeologists during a dig in Xi'an, China, in 2023, the oldest known flush-toilets in the world date to around 400 BCE. Bog boffins believe this toilet was warmed by an emperor and flushed manually by servants.

Most expensive

An 18-carat gold toilet worth £4.8m ($6m) was part of a participatory art project (punters were encouraged to use it) at Blenheim Palace in Oxfordshire, England, until it was stolen. However, the most expensive toilet ever was in Hang Fung Gold Technology's showroom in Hong Kong – made with 24-carat gold and coated with gems, it was worth some $29m.

Toilets of the World
October 2025
Published by Lonely Planet Global Limited
CRN: 554153
ISBN: 9781837585847
© Lonely Planet 2025
10 9 8 7 6 5 4 3 2 1
Printed in Malaysia

Publishing Director Piers Pickard
Publisher, Gift & Illustrated Becca Hunt
Senior Editor Robin Barton
Editor Polly Thomas
Written by Patrick Kinsella
Art Director / Designer Emily Dubin
Layout Designer Jo Dovey
Image Researcher Heike Bohnstengel
Mapping Wayne Murphy
Print Production Nigel Longuet

STAY IN TOUCH
lonelyplanet.com/contact

Lonely Planet Office:
Digital Depot, Roe Lane (off Thomas St), Digital Hub, Dublin 8, D08 TCV4, IRELAND

Front Cover: Nordic Images/Alamy, Ureddplassen, Norwegian Scenic Route Helgelandskysten, Architect: Haugen/Zohar Arkitekter; **Back Cover:** Tony Rowell/Getty Images, wewi-creative/Shutterstock, Robert Coolen/Shutterstock; **3:** Vova Shevchuk/Shutterstock; **4:** Xinhua/Shutterstock; **5:** Universal History Archive/Getty Images, Pictures from History/Getty Images; **6:** Wikimedia Commons; **7:** Wikimedia Commons, Guy BOUCHET/Getty Images; **10:** imageBROKER.com GmbH & Co. KG/Alamy; **11:** Stephen Dorey Creative/Alamy; **12:** Andreas von Einsiedel/Alamy; **13:** blickwinkel/B. Trapp/Alamy; **15:** Robin Weaver/Alamy; **16:** Keith J Smith/Alamy; **17:** wewi-creative/Shutterstock; **18:** Jürgen Wiesler/Alamy; **19:** Andreas von Einsiedel/Alamy; **20:** imageBROKER.com GmbH & Co. KG/Alamy; **22:** Ingrid Pakats/Shutterstock; **23:** Roger Coulam/Alamy; **24:** allan wright/Alamy; **25:** Irine and Andrew/Shutterstock; Toilets at Dyrhólaey natural reserve, South Iceland, by GLÁMA KÍM architects (www.glamakim.is). Client: The Environment Agency of Iceland; **27:** robert coolen/Shutterstock; **28:** Natallia Khlapushyna/Alamy; **29:** Steve Vidler/mauritius images GmbH/Alamy; **30:** James Balston/Arcaid Images/Alamy; **31:** eddie linssen/Alamy; **32:** Udo Siebig/mauritius images GmbH /Alamy; **34:** Erik Laan/Shutterstock; **35:** Christopher Moswitzer/Shutterstock; **36:** Yuri Turkov/Alamy; **37:** hans engbers/Shutterstock; **39:** FotoHelin/Shutterstock; **40:** Nathaniel Noir/Alamy; **44:** ADS/Alamy; **45:** Wolfgang Zwanzger/

YAY Media AS /Alamy; **46:** YAY Media AS/Alamy; **47:** Edwin Tan/Getty Images; **49:** De Klerk/Alamy; **50:** Dmitriy Feldman svarshik/Shutterstock; **51:** Bill Gozansky/Alamy; **52:** Juergen_Wallstabe/Shutterstock; **53:** Olga Gordeeva/Shutterstock; **54:** Westend61/Getty Images; **56:** Andrey Nekrasov/Shutterstock; **57:** Pmmrd/Shutterstock; **58:** Craig Lovell/Eagle Visions Photography/Alamy; **59:** Sergey Strelkov/Getty Images; **60:** Matyas Rehak/Alamy; **61:** Juha Puikkonen/Alamy; **65:** Ned Snowman/Shutterstock; **66:** Pio3/Shutterstock; **67:** anouchka/Getty Images; **68:** Eric Dodson/Alamy; **70:** Danita Delimont/Alamy; **71:** Imaginechina Limited/Alamy; **72:** Wirestock/Alamy; **73:** Sipa US/Alamy; **75:** Ivan Effendy/Alamy; **76:** John Lander/Alamy; **77:** wimammoth/Shutterstock; **78:** Jürgen Wiesler/imageBROKER.com GmbH & Co. KG/Alamy; **79:** Andreas Körner/mauritius images GmbH/Alamy; **80:** My Golden life/Shutterstock; **82:** Marek Slusarczyk/Alamy; **83:** Zvonimir Atletic/Shutterstock; **84:** angeluisma/Getty Images; **85:** blickwinkel/B. Trapp/Alamy; **87:** Gairah foto/Shutterstock; **88:** Maciej Bledowski/Shutterstock; **89:** Nina Ross/Shutterstock; **90:** John W W/Shutterstock; **91:** Al.geba/Shutterstock; **92:**

Evaldas Mikoliunas/Alamy; **94:** Anadolu/Getty Images; **98:** Annalucia/Alamy; **99:** domonabike/Alamy; **100:** Geoff Marshall/Alamy; **101:** Andy Selinger/Alamy; **103:** Steve Jordan/Stockimo/Alamy; **104:** Ian Crocker/Shutterstock; **105:** dave stamboulis/Alamy; **106:** Andrea Robinson/Getty Images; **107:** Paul Harding 00/Shutterstock; **108:** MattTaylor92/Shutterstock; **112:** Ira Berger/Alamy; **113:** SF photo/Shutterstock; **114:** EWY Media/Alamy; **115:** Michele and Tom Grimm/Alamy; **117:** Martha Almeyda/Shutterstock; **118:** Danny Ye/Shutterstock; **119:** Matthew Micah Wright/Getty Images; **120:** Simon Grosset/Alamy; **121:** steve waters/Alamy; **122:** Tony Rowell/Getty Images; **124:** dave stamboulis/Alamy; **125:** Fred Hirschmann/RGB Ventures/SuperStock /Alamy; **126:** Travis J. Camp/Shutterstock; **127:** Uwe Moser/Getty Images; **129:** Matyas Rehak/Shutterstock; **130:** Graham Prentice/Alamy; **131:** Chris Howarth/Bolivia/Alamy; **132:** Ashley Molitor/Getty Images; **133:** Santiago Urquijo/Getty Images; **134:** Radius Images/Design Pics/Alamy; **136:** Joshua Rainey/Getty Images; **137:** Mikadun/Shutterstock; **138:** Danielle Alling/Shutterstock; **139:** FORGET Patrick/Alamy; **141:** Jon Bower/Alamy; **143:** Sipa Asia/Shutterstock